A playbook containing modern day words and wisdom for guys starting their journey to manhood.

Have You Filled His Backpack?

Elizabeth Kokalis

BackPack Publishing

Backpack Publishing LLC
Oak Creek, Wisconsin
backpackpublishing@gmail.com

Dream...Write...Inspire...Do it!

ISBN: 978-0-9963899-2-1

Disclaimer: The author and publisher do not assume any responsibility for
any outcomes as a result of the contents written, unless they are positive.
This book is written to inspire thoughts and conversations. If expert
assistance or counseling is needed, seek the help of a professional. The
reader should take everything written with a grain of sugar.

Cover design and book layout by Clifford Krebs.

Photos including cover photo purchased by depositphoto.com using
standard licensing agreement with the exception of the boy stretching
which is the author's personal photo.

To Leo and Amalia

The Road Trip

(Contents)

Thank you to my friends and loved ones.
(You know who you are).

Introduction

The first book *Have You Filled Her Backpack?* was written for girls but, to my surprise, I found out that boys and men were equally interested, curious and wanted to read the book secretly and sometimes openly. Some snippet information, words of wisdom and advice apply to both guys and girls; however, there are some differences that I needed to address specifically for guys because, as you know, boys are different than girls.

We sometimes don't have time to put pen to paper to describe what we want to share. This book is a vehicle to bring back some old values with the young men living in a high tech and fast paced society. Much like the girls version it is written to inspire conversations. Boys, however, may want to read it by themselves, create their opinions and when the time is right have a conversation.

The book provides practical advice to give young men the confidence in some uncharted waters, to be successful in whatever they pursue as they start their lives into adulthood. It's also a life boat to resuscitate chivalry, because... it's not dead, but it is on life support. Dad and grandpa may have done these chivalrous acts and they may still be doing them today without giving it a second thought. The question is: have our young boys developed and picked up and those tips and way of life? Will they grow up to become a gentleman? I have included a chapter on Dating and Chivalry. It will introduce some helpful thoughts as a guide of gentlemanly gestures. Just as the original book, I start the first chapter with daily rituals. The second chapter is on health and exercise. The third chapter is for *his* fashion and the grooming arsenal. The book concludes with some additional thoughts for guys in the catch all collection chapter that didn't fit in any other category.

So, why wait? Let's start filling his backpack!

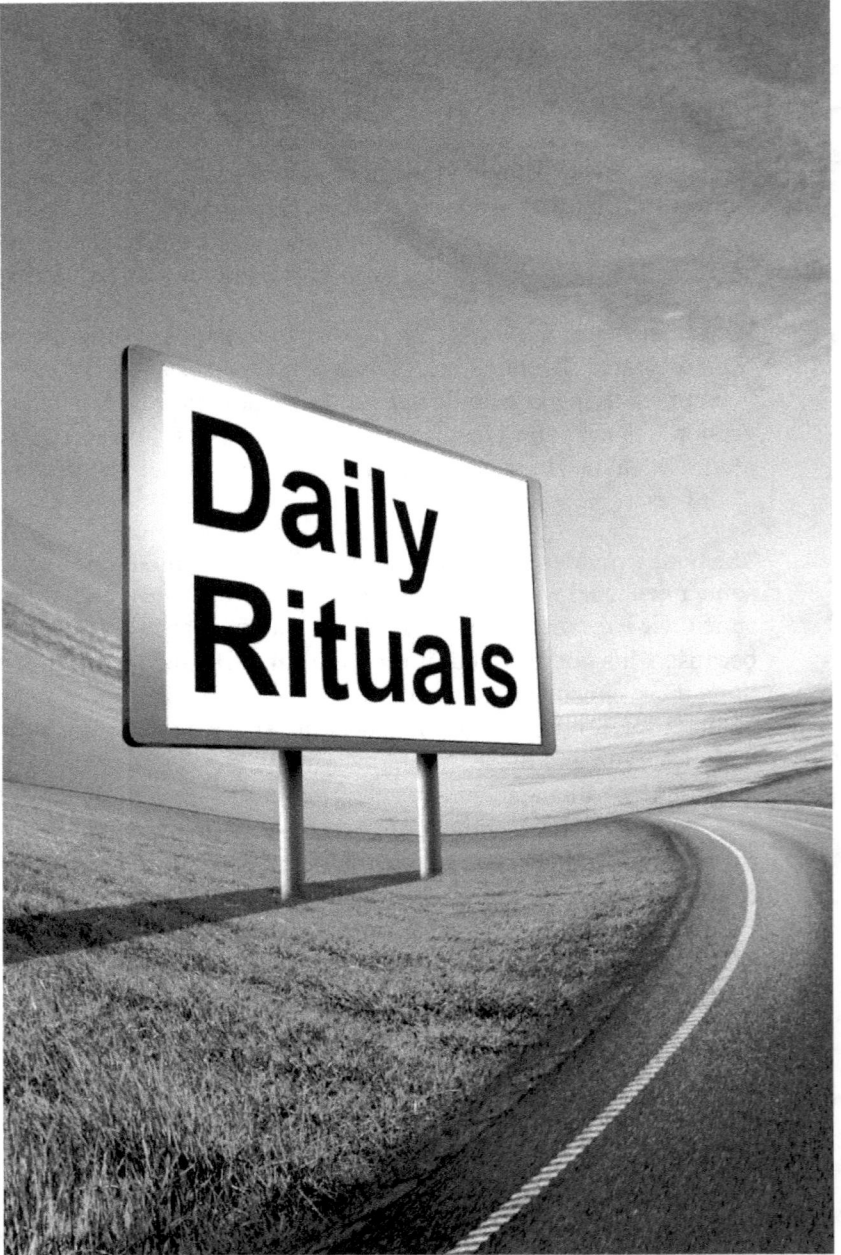

CHAPTER 1

Wish people a "good morning". It's a wonderful way to start your day and theirs too.

Remember to brush and floss your teeth.

Most guys will shave when they get out of the shower. After showering the face is hydrated and makes it a closer shave. Oh, and don't forget to clean the sink.

Take a few minutes to make your bed. It's your first accomplishment of the day. It can set the tone of your day in a positive way.

Always lift the seat up and try to have good aim; otherwise please clean up after yourself. Remember, it's polite to always put the toilet seat down when finished.

Stay healthy: wash your hands often.

See problems as opportunities for growth.

Have a good pair of shoes to walk and work in.

Remember not to salt your food before you taste it.
Why? It could be an indication that you assume things are a certain way;
that you perhaps make decisions without having all the information. Not to
mention insulting the chef or cook that he hasn't seasoned your meal.
There have been old stories or tales circulating for years that famous
executives took applicants interviewing for a job out to lunch and observed
whether they salted their food or not before taking their first bite. If they
did salt before tasting they were not hired.

Keep a running "to do list". It helps you be organized and remember what
you need to get done. It'll be good practice for when you get older and have
a "honey do list" given to you by your significant other.

Write timely thank you notes.

Trust your intuition or "gut" feelings.

Read, Read, Read
Feed, Feed, Feed
Your mind....

Learn about politics, world and current affairs.

Laugh whenever you can: it feels great.

Remember that nothing good happens after midnight.

When you are going for a run or walking in the street, always face towards the direction of oncoming traffic. It sounds strange, but you can see the cars coming.

Pick out your clothes the night before; it saves time in the morning.

Make good decisions and choices.

Remember to wear sunscreen, sunburn hurts and too much sun causes wrinkles later in life.

The elders have wisdom; listen to them.

"Pan Metron Ariston"
Translation: Everything in moderation.
(An unknown ancient Greek philosopher)

Listen to and appreciate a variety of music.

Think before you speak and know when to keep your mouth closed.

Speak your mind, but do it respectfully.

Celebrate the little things in life: completing a tough project, waking up to the spring aroma of lilacs, wearing your favorite jacket and finding money in the pockets, or receiving unexpected hugs and kisses from a loved one.

Be honest but never hurtful.
Always think of how it would make you feel to hear
something unpleasant about yourself.

If you don't ask the question; you'll never know the answer.

Happiness is a choice; it's a setting in your mind that you can adjust.

It may be instinctual but still worth mentioning.

Public Restroom Protocol:

- Typically you don't greet or have a conversation with anyone while you're in there.
- If you can, leave a buffer between you and others.
- Look straight ahead, down or up, and no side peeking.
- Remember to zip up your fly.
- It's important to wash your hands and then use a paper towel or elbow to open the door on your way out.

Basically, guys get in and get out unlike women who like to chit chat.

Be positive, stay positive and you will attract the positive in your life. No one likes to be around negativity; it only breeds more negative feelings in people. Therefore, surround yourself with positive people.

Practice random acts of kindness; it's a blast to do and people won't expect it.

Be kind, gentle and loving.

Don't swear or use the f- bomb; it can be offensive to others. There are more intelligent words to use to get your point across.

Timing is everything and having patience is important.
You might not get the results you want if you don't time your actions.

You are sometimes judged by the company you keep.
Have you heard of guilt by association?

Try not to waste time and energy on things that may not happen.

If you want to walk and listen to your iPod, use only one ear bud.
You can't hear what is happening around you, or if someone comes
up behind if you have both buds in.

Don't take things for granted. Instead, count your blessings.

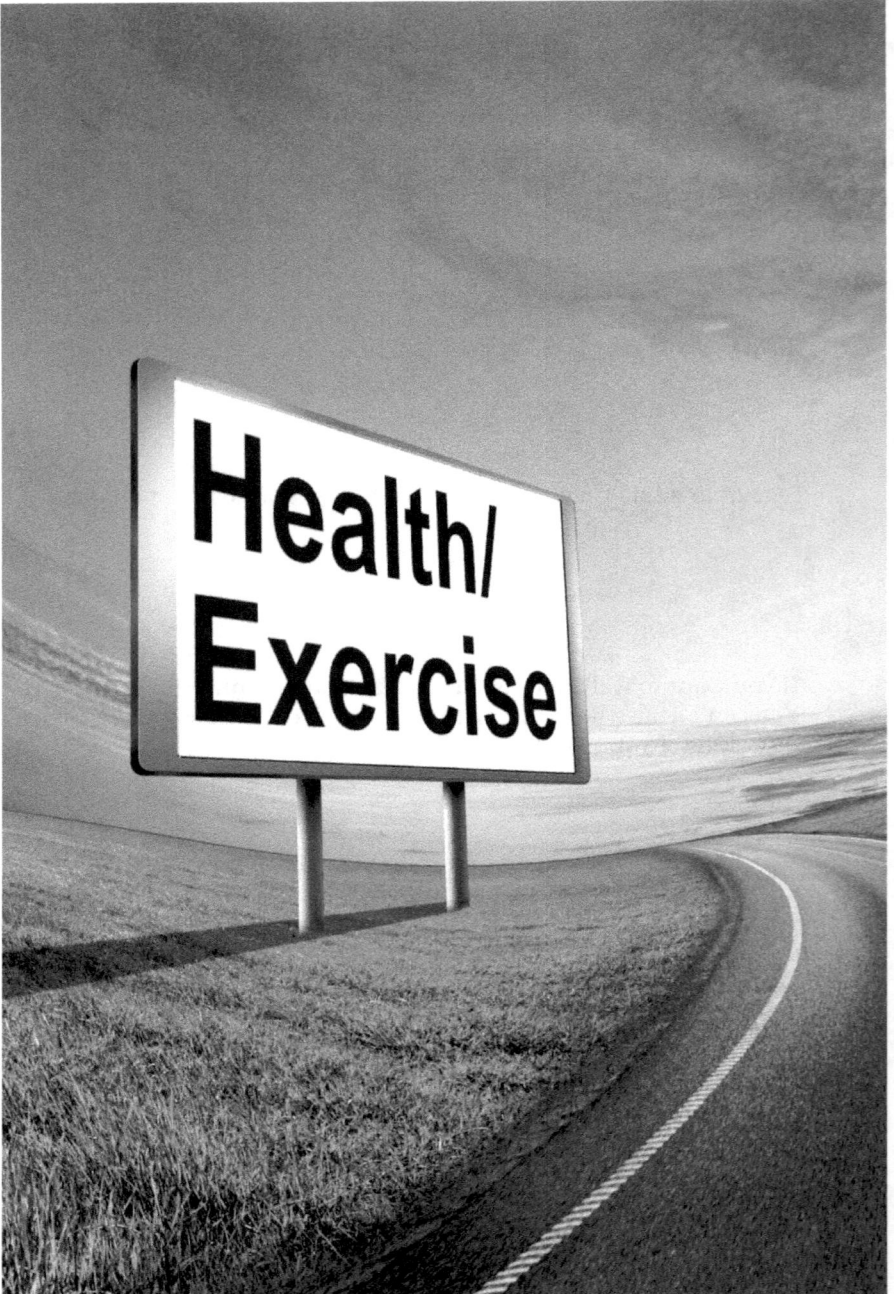

CHAPTER 2

Alcohol may be a solution in chemistry,
but it's only a temporary one in life.

If you work out at the gym, wipe the sweat off the equipment.

Try balancing weight lifting with some cardio activity.

Change up your exercise routine not to reach a plateau. Plateau means
remaining stable and not progressing.

You don't need a gym membership to exercise. You can do push- ups at
home, go for run, a walk or ride your bike.

Don't smoke; it quickly becomes an expensive habit and it's very difficult to quit.

Don't do drugs. They are illegal and you could go to jail.
This would change your life forever.
Note: "Not inhaling" is still participating.

When you turn 21 have a drink but drink responsibly.

Heavy drinking can age your face.
It speeds up the aging process on your skin, causing early wrinkles.
The consumption of large quantities of alcohol dehydrates your body;
and the hydration is required for youthful skin.

Try a meditation class once in your life.

Be focused and disciplined.

There are benefits in going to bed at the same time every night. It sets a routine and makes it easier to get up in the morning.

Overeating is not healthy and neither is under eating. If you are concerned about your eating habits don't wait too long to talk to someone about it.

Try every day to drink half of your body weight in water by converting your weight into ounces from pounds. For example, if you weigh 130 pounds, you would drink 65 ounces of water daily. Drinking a lot of water can helps control calories and replaces fluids lost during exercise.

Do some stretching daily to be fit.

Have breakfast; it helps kick start your brain function.

Eating protein rich foods daily is important for your diet. Protein helps your body repair cells among other things.
Protein rich foods are: nuts, eggs, chicken, beef, pork or fish.

Eat fruits and vegetables every day. There are many to choose from. Find some you like. Healthy habits start when you're young.

Try to make fish part of your weekly diet. It's packed with protein and nutrients. If you don't like the taste of fish, dip it in ketchup. Almost everything tastes better with ketchup.

If you have a doctor's appointment, write a list of questions in advance that you would like to ask.

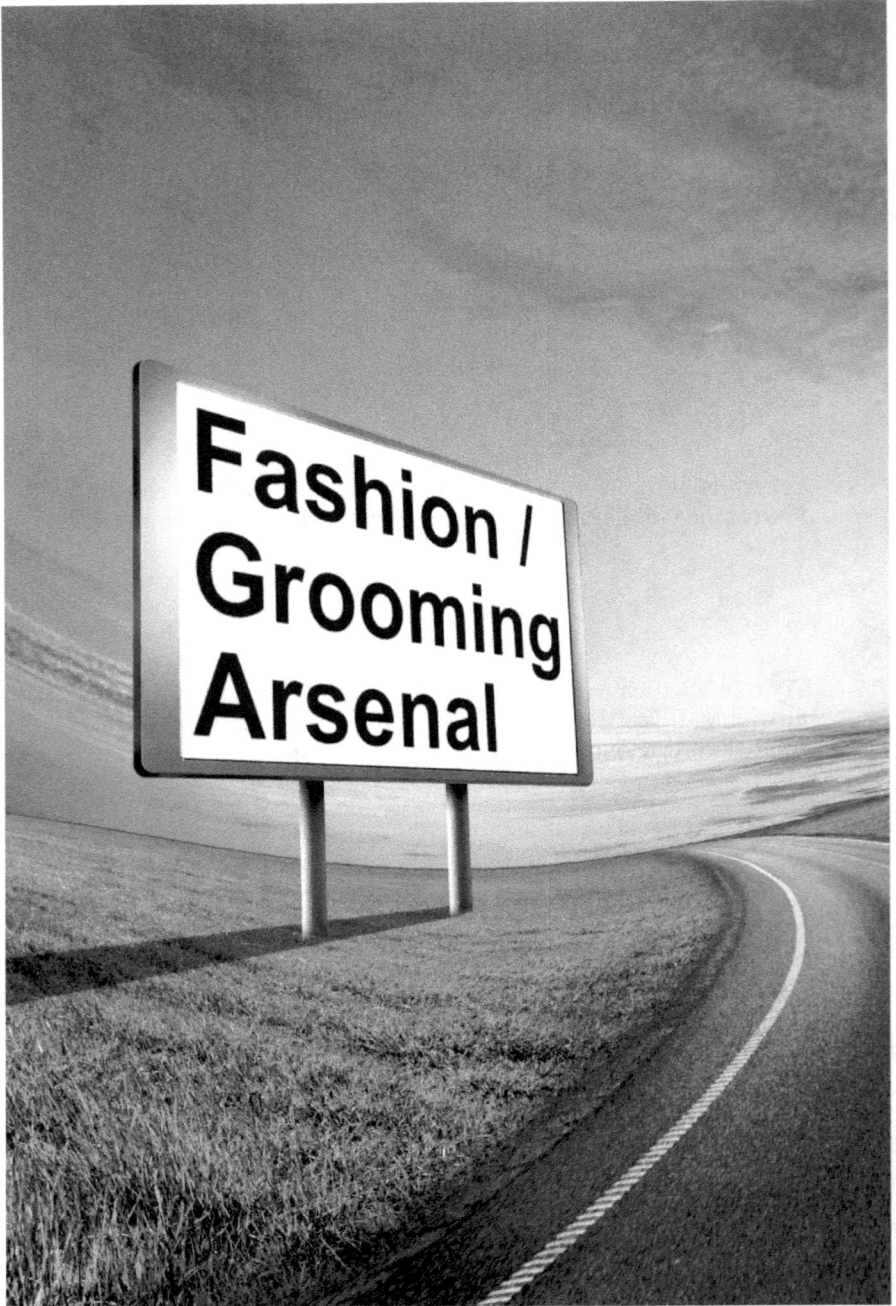

CHAPTER 3

Fashion /
Grooming
Arsenal

A guy who cares about his appearance is much more attractive than a sloppy dressed dude. Wearing jeans and a shirt is good look; however, sometimes you need to dress for the occasion.

Here is a list of must have items to start a guy's wardrobe:

- One white and colored dress shirt
- One tie.
- One sports coat
- Dress socks and dress shoes
- One pair of blue or black dress slacks
- A belt
- One sweater
- Leather jacket and a wool coat is a must have
- Eventually try to own a nice suit

A suit can be worn to a wedding or a funeral. It also can be worn to a job interview (depending on the job you're interviewing for). You need to dress a step up from what the job requires as a dress code. For example, if you are interviewing for a delivery job you wouldn't need to wear a suit. You could wear a nice pair of cargo pants and shirt.

Skip the white socks when wearing dress shoes or sandals please.

When wearing a suit in a standing position leave it buttoned.
When you sit down, unbutton it.

If you feel good about yourself you will look good too.

Sometimes what you wear determines your mood and how you feel.

Remember to wear an undershirt (not a muscle t-shirt), especially when wearing a button down dress shirt. Undershirts come in different colors if you don't like the standard white issue. Your shirts will last longer because it absorbs perspiration and prevents deodorant stains. If you have a hairy chest it may prevent hair sticking through your shirts. Wearing an undershirt also gives you another layer of warmth.

It's not attractive to wear your pants hanging off your butt.

Remember to use deodorant.

Dress pants should be worn at your waist not below your belly.
A belt should also be worn with your dress pants.

Business casual usually means khakis and a shirt with a collar.

Boxer or briefs? Either way replace when needed.

If you have a unibrow, have the barber pluck, wax, or straight razor it.

If you use a wallet, don't over stuff it with receipts and useless stuff.

If you decide to wear any style of beard or mustache, keep it trimmed and groomed.

Have clean and trimmed nails.

Guys too can use lotion on their hands.

To dress up your jeans, a classy and sharp look could be wearing a sports jacket with your jeans.

Color-code your closet to find items easier. You can organize your closet by dark colors to light colors with all other colors in between.
Try using plastic hangers and face all clothes the same direction.

If you buy a new shirt, pair of pants or pair of shoes,
let another item go from your closet.
Practice the one- in- one- out rule.
(This rule is a way to have control of things you own and to avoid clutter)

Donate your old clothes. It can make a difference in someone's life.
Consider donating to a shelter or other charitable organizations.

Own a clothing iron and ironing board.

Don't pop your zits. Your fingers, no matter how clean, have bacteria on
them and make it worse.

Chapter 4

Dining etiquette varies by country and culture.
(When in Rome be a Roman).

If you're attending a formal dinner that has multiple eating utensils, start using the utensils placed the farthest on either side of the plate.

The spoon and fork above your plate are usually used for dessert. Good rule of thumb, use whichever makes the most sense; the fork for cake and spoon for ice-cream.

When eating with one or more people, wait until everyone has been served before you start eating.

What to do with the napkin? Well, place it on your lap. Don't stuff it on the top of your shirt. When you're finished with your meal, nicely fold it and place it to the left of your plate.

It's not polite to reach across the table or over a person for anything. Ask for it to be passed to you. Food should be passed counter clockwise or to your right in American style of dining.

"Excuse me; can you please pass me the salt?"
The salt and pepper should be passed
"as a pair."

If you don't wish to have what's in the bowl being passed to you, say thank you and keep passing the bowl; don't put it down.
Keep the train moving.

If you are served soup, scoop with the spoon away from you. Never pick up the cup or bowl and slurp the remaining soup unless the culture dictates it. In Japan, slurping the remaining soup is a sign it was delicious. However, this is not acceptable in other Asian cultures, and especially not in the USA.

Don't cut all your meat up at once. Cut only 1-2 bite sized pieces at a time. Place your knife down and continue using the hand you normally eat with. Repeat until you are finished eating. This is the American style of dining. It is also referred to as the cut and switch style.

European countries use the Continental style of dining. It seems more practical. They hold the fork in one hand and keep the knife in the other hand never switching the utensils back and forth. They cut and eat, cut and eat.

Are you wondering what to do with the bread?
Surprisingly, you break it up into pieces. Place a small amount of butter on your plate and butter only what you are ready to eat.

Remember elbows off the table.
However, if you travel to Russia, rest your wrists on the dinner table so they are visible.

What's sorbet?
It's like a fruity frozen slushy with a little thicker consistency;
everyone's dream!
It's actually served to cleanse and refresh your palate for the next course.

When you're dining in a restaurant, if the silverware falls off the table don't look for it or pick it up. You can pretend like it never happened and ask the server for a new one.

In some countries like China, Turkey and parts of the Middle East, a big belch after a good meal indicates it was delicious and is a compliment to the chef.

It's fun to learn some toasts in other languages. Some of the same toasts are used by several countries. Here is a list of a few of them: Prost (German), Nazdravie (Polish), Ziveli (Serbian), Lech aim (Hebrew), Gan bai (Chinese), Ya mas (Greek), Salud (Spanish), Cin-Cin (Italian), and Viva (Brazilian).

If you are invited to dinner at someone's house, always bring a small gift
like flowers, dessert, or something homemade.
When you turn 21 years old a bottle of wine is also appropriate.
It's the gesture that counts.
Note: Don't buy the cheap stuff; you may have to drink it too!

When on a date at a nice restaurant pull the chair out for the girl and then
slowly push the chair in while she is lowering down to sit.

Throughout the world, the one commonality we all share is that a meal
brings us together.

bon appetite, buon appetito, guten appetit, buen provecho,
kali orexi, or enjoy your meal!

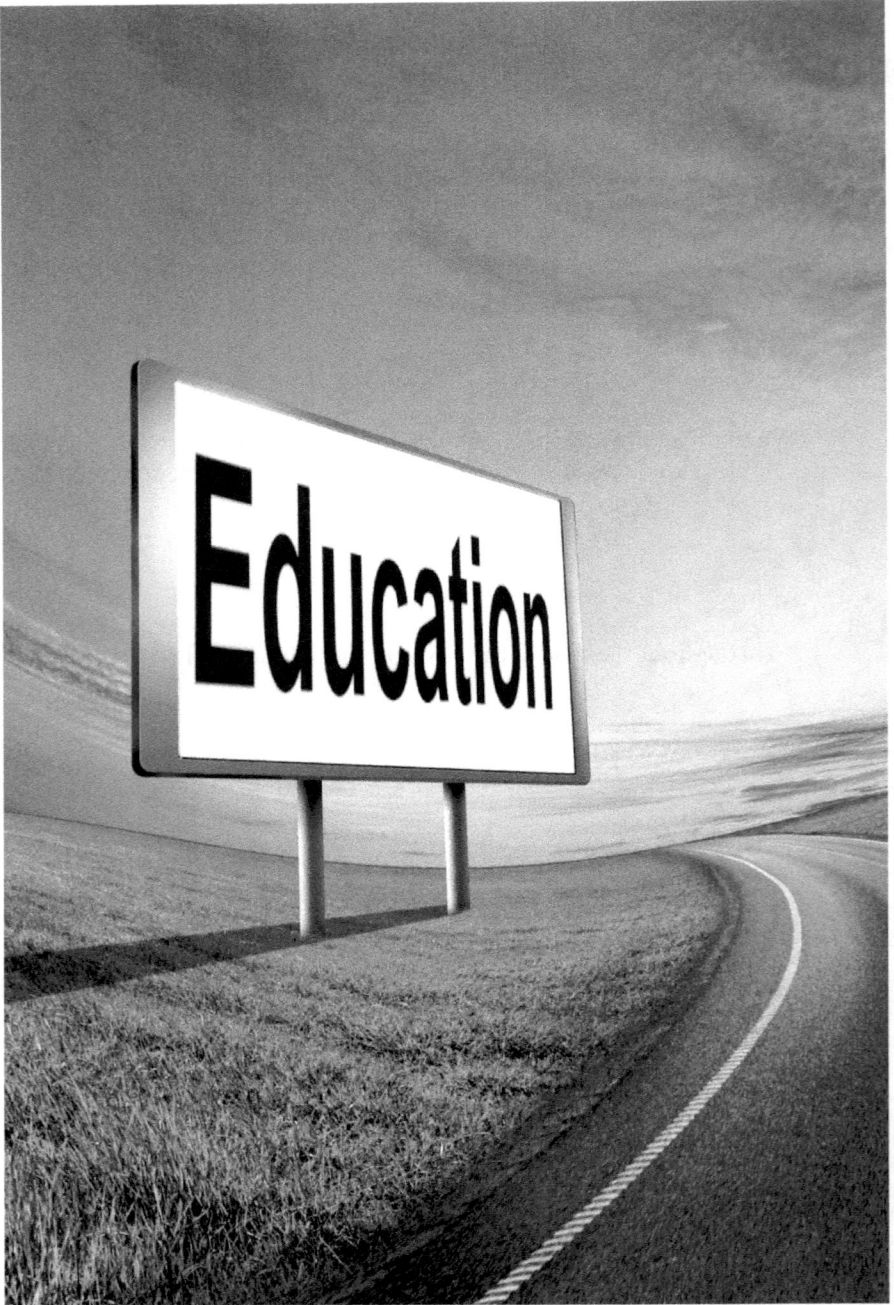

CHAPTER 5

Get an education! It's something that no one can ever take away from you.

If you feel you may not be cut out to go to a four year university. There are community colleges that offer many career studies. It's a less expensive alternative if you are unsure of your career path.
Note: There is a high demand for skilled tradesmen. Some of the skilled trades are welders, plumbers, masons and electricians.

Your first semester of college will be challenging. It's a new school, new environment, possible new roommates and teachers that have higher expectations. You'll be okay.

When in class or at a seminar, always try to sit in front.
You are there to learn.

Professors while teaching like to also provide their personal opinions or points of view; take in the information, but create your own opinions.

Avoid the fearful "freshman 15" by exercising and eating healthy meals and snacks.

College is the some of the best years of your life; find your balance.
When you're in college, you have to manage your time between classes,
studying, work, friends and activities. Earning good grades is very
important. College life is a juggling act requiring balance.

College can be stressful. Make sure you have a network
of people you can to talk if you need encouragement.

Know that a student charged with a drug related offense could lose
the financial aid they received.

School comes first before going out with your friends.
Be focused and stay on course.

Strive to be able to support yourself.

Be a perpetual student of knowledge.

"Strong minds discuss ideas,
Average minds discuss events,
Weak minds discuss people."
~Socrates

Try to be well-rounded in your conversations.

Be the best at everything you do; it will make you feel good
at the end of the day.

Make new friends that you share common interests with and maybe even
consider starting a study group.

Join a club.

Having a variety of knowledge is power and strength.
Note: It's also helpful when you're playing board games.

Study..... Study..... Study!

Sleep is very important: you need to rest your body and mind.

When learning and memorizing new material find techniques that help you recall and retain information: using acronyms, word associations, creating a song/story, or making flash cards.

Reviewing material before bedtime is a secret way to retain information.

Cramming for a test may be good for the short run; it's not good for long term retention of information. Reviewing material daily is best.

You should try to unplug yourself from the stimulation your electronics provide for at least one hour a day. This means take a break from your cell phone and social media. Your phone and computer like your brain needs to recharge; otherwise you can't use it effectively.

Be curious and ask questions.

C's get degrees in the short term! Things may change in your life and you might need to switch careers and this may require going back to school. You may have to provide your high school or college transcripts. If you got C's you may not be able to get into the school or the trade. So, do your best now because you can't go back and do a retake.

"Whatever is good to know is difficult to learn."
~Greek Proverb
(Don't give up.)

Apply for scholarships: it could be a way to lower your tuition.

Be aware of deadlines and be sure you don't miss them.

"Successful people are not afraid to think."
~Daniel V. Gonzalez

CHAPTER 6

Finding a job is a job in itself.

Have confidence in yourself.

Subscribe to LinkedIn and start networking.
You could be exposed to people who may have a connection you need.

When using someone as a reference, always ask the person for their permission first. Remember to consider past teachers and coaches as possible referees.

Prepare an elevator speech on who you are.
An elevator speech is a 30 second summary of who you are and what you like to do. The speech is called this way in reference to the time span of riding in an elevator and, of course, always facing forward.

Think about how you would be an asset
to the company you are applying to.

Be prepared. Do some research on the company you are interviewing with and maybe even mention a well-known fact. Also, they might ask you questions to see what you know about the company.

Employers like a team player, and a person who is honest and ethical.

Think of stories ahead of time that you could cite to support your answer to interviewing questions.

During your interview don't use slang or texting language like LOL.

It's important to make eye contact during the interviewer.

Don't forget to bring several copies of your resume along and have it readily available.

Have a few questions for you to ask the interviewer.

Read and remember the company's "mission statement".

Dress nicely and appropriately.

Be on time or even a few minutes early for your interview.

Have a firm handshake.

Don't chew gum.

Remember not to fold your arms.

Stand up straight and don't slouch.

Remember to smile!

Know it's not inappropriate to ask what the starting wage is.

Don't ramble on. Be concise in your answers.

Explain how you have what it takes to do the job.
Sell yourself; it's your time to shine!

Thank your interviewer for their time.

Don't post on social media about your interview.

Send the interviewer a thank you via email.
It may seem outdated, but also send your interviewer
a hand written thank you note.

CHAPTER 7

Have a professional photo taken every few years to keep up with your new look and maturity. You never know when you will need it.

Become familiar with the 80/20 Rule or the Pareto Principal.
This concept can also be applied to your job or career;
20% of the people do 80% of the work.
Be the 20%!

Dress for the job you want, not the one you have.

Never take credit for someone else's work.

Your work can define you; chose what you like and enjoy doing.

Receiving a promotion in a job is earned, not given.

If you have an idea or an invention- follow your dreams. You CAN become an entrepreneur. Learn what P/L (profit and loss) means, because you need to be profitable to stay in business.
Note: not everyone can be a Jeff Bezos of Amazon.

Things will get tough, and you will need to pull out your "game face" and get focused.

Take pride in your work.

Never compromise your integrity.
"Integrity is doing the right thing when no one is watching."
~ C.S. Lewis

Keep an on-going list of your achievements or successes when time comes for your review and a raise in pay. That way, you will have feedback and documentation for your boss or supervisor. This can be a letter of praise someone sent you about the good job you've done, a thank you email someone sent, a positive survey comment or a suggestion that you have made which was incorporated.

Know your loyalties and keep them.

HAVE YOU FILLED HIS BACKPACK?

Have big goals and break them down into smaller goals so you can achieve them and not feel frustrated about how long it could potentially take to reach the big goal. This can be for work or your personal life.
Reward yourself along the way.

Write your goals down. If you don't, they don't count.

Don't accept being average.

Be a leader, not a follower.
If everyone was a leader would there be followers?
Yes, because some people can only follow.

Prepare the night before for the work you do the following day.

Try to make a difference.

Be clever and creative.

It's easier to find a new job if you already have one.

If you ever want to complain, you chose the job or career you have.
Try not to be afraid to change it if you can.
~Amalia Melissourgos

53

CHAPTER 8

Seek out the good in people.

Remember: make the bed when you are an overnight guest in someone's home.

Try to see things from other people's points of view; especially in politics or religion.

Don't burn any bridges. You might have to cross the same river some day in the future. It's easier for you to cross that bridge if it's still standing.

Pay attention not to play the blame game seek understanding instead.

Guys will look at other women. It's in the DNA.
However, a GENTLEMAN never gets caught looking and would never do it in front of his girlfriend or any girl he is with.

55

Some successful girls may seem tough and intimidating.
Know that they are not always tough on the inside.

If and when you decide to have sex and it's before marriage, USE protection. Participating in a girl becoming pregnant is an important decision and should not be made in the heat of the moment. Remember you are financially responsible for your child until the child is 18 years old, sometimes beyond 18 years old. You are also responsible for them emotionally. You will have a life time bond with the other parent as well.

Learn to be a good listener. Don't always try to solve problems.

"Don't just look at the flower. Look at the seed."
~Elias Kokalis

Boys and men when in a relationship can find other women attractive. Please don't make it obvious and don't act on an impulse. If you love your girl, you would not want to hurt her by cheating on her or making a fool of yourself. It's a conscious choice you make not to act on impulse.

Know the number of girlfriends you have is not as important as the quality of the relationship with each girlfriend.

The person after a break-up who feels the most rejection and displays resentment and anger is the one who possibly feels the most hurt or is the most insecure.

Most women want a man to make her feel safe and secure.

Treat your girlfriend the way you would want your sister to be treated by her boyfriend.

When choosing a girlfriend pay attention on how she treats strangers, her parents and how she treats friends.

Girls like to be told that they are pretty or beautiful. You may think that she may only need to hear it once; know that she likes to hear more often.

Most girls love to talk. Silence makes them feel uncomfortable. They may feel like you are not interested if you're not engaged in conversation all the time. You can try to explain to her that silence is not always negative. It's relaxing to have quite time.

"One-nighters" or one night stands are
one time sex without emotional commitment.
"Casual sex" can be regular sex with friends.
This is also known as "friends with benefits". It's no "strings attached" sex.
There is no romantic involvement or a future of a committed relationship.

Do you really want that?

People's actions speak louder than words.
The two are sometimes not in sync.
This is why you need to pay attention to
not only their words but actions

There is a difference between flirting and being friendly with others.
Your intentions and desired outcome will define which of the two you and
others are doing.

Reserve your kisses for the person who you are in a relationship with.
Kiss the person you care about on the cheek, not the lips.

There are two types of jealousy: unhealthy and healthy.

People who display unwarranted jealousy in a relationship may be insecure, have fear of abandonment or want to control. Some repeated behaviors of unhealthy jealousy can be: constantly and obsessively checking up on you by calling several times a day to ask where you are, spying when you are out with your friends, looking at your phones text messages daily or questioning why you are a few minutes late coming home. He/she may even demand you don't spend time with your other friends.

Healthy jealousy, on the other hand, is normal when there is a real threat or uncertainty to your relationship. You need to address any feelings of jealousy or insecurities in your relationship right away.

A man will stand up for and girl who is being disrespected or in danger.

If you end a relationship always try to make it a kind and a loving ending.

Family comes before your friends, unless your friends are your family.

If you want good friends, you have to be a good friend.

Keep a few good friends no matter what the distance.

A good friend wants you to be happy and is happy for you.

Please don't let your friends drive drunk; give them a ride or call them a taxi cab or Uber.

When you are not with your significant other, don't do anything (i.e. flirt) you would not do in front of her.

Relationships are like an investment: if you are not getting enough interest, move on...

Your first break up is hard.
Well, all break ups are hard but you will get through it.
Most think that their first love is their only love and they could never possibly love again. Have faith, there is someone out there for you, and you will love again. Use the time alone to become comfortable with who you are and what you want before you start a relationship again.

Don't think you can change someone because you can't.
You can only change yourself.

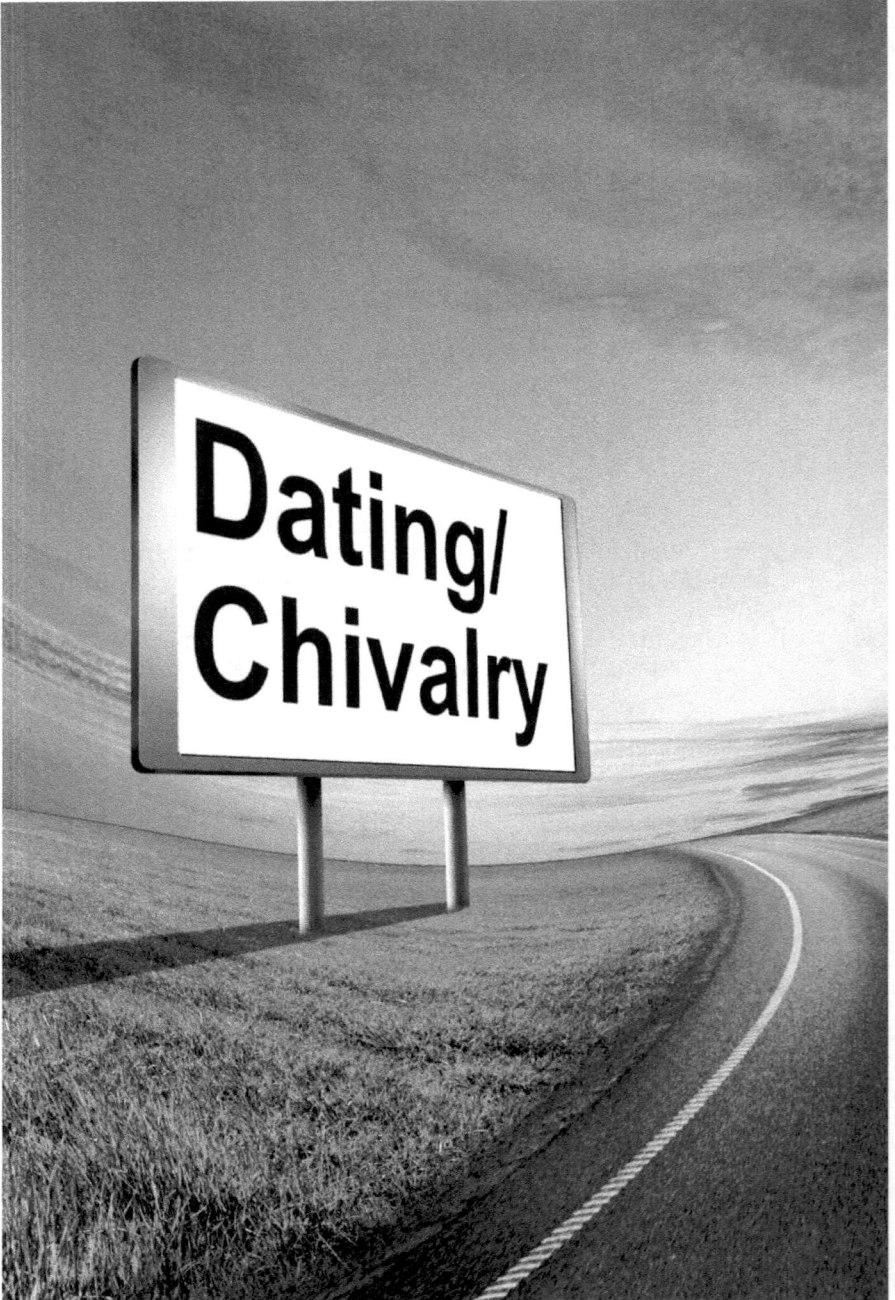

CHAPTER 9

Manners= Chivalry

Girls are capable of doing things on their own (and some won't hesitate telling you), but most girls deep down like to be treated like a lady and have the guys be guys. Just because it's the 21st century some things are still timeless. Being a gentleman may set you apart from the rest of the guys. Chivalrous acts should not be done to impress but rather a way to conduct your life. It shows you have manners and are kind considerate guy.

Girls who work and/or have careers are sometimes not accustomed to guys being chivalrous because they may work in a dog eat dog world. They have to fight to survive and get ahead. They become assertive and aggressive. It frequently bleeds into their personal lives unconsciously. Those may be the girls that require a gentleman.

Dating can be one or more of the following:

- Going to the prom, the movies, a party, or a wedding.
- A guy asks a girl out to dinner or some type of event; for example, concert or sporting game. (Or the girl asks the guy).
- Meeting socially for companionship and friendship.
- Exploring if you are compatible with each other by having long conversations over a cup of coffee.

Ending a date can be uncomfortable or awkward. You might not be sure if you should kiss her. It gets easier after a few dates. It's always safe to kiss her on the check or to give her a hug. She will let you know how she feels by the response you get back. Note: A date doesn't have to end with a sexual encounter.

Open the door for a girl, women or the elderly walking into a building.

Walk a girl to her car, especially if it's late and dark outside and then have the girl drive you to your car.

When on a date open the car door for her.

When going with her to a party, it pays to know how to dance.

Try to be romantic; most girls like that, but only do it if you are sincere.

Getting caught walking in the rain on a warm summer night with your girlfriend can be romantic.

Most girls are impressed by a guy who can cook at least 1-2 meals. It's also a healthier and cheaper alternative then going out to eat all the time.

Don't "lead" a girl on by giving her ambiguous promises; be honest with her.

It's a nice gesture to offer your jacket to girl who is cold.

If you're on your way to a formal event (like a wedding) and it's pouring down rain, it can be an act of chivalry to offer to bring the car around for her.

Don't become the guy who brags and keeps a running list of girls they have slept with. It's also not impressive or cool to share that with your date.

Be a man with morals.

When you are walking with a girl, have her walk on the inside. In other words you walk closer to the street. It's a feeling of protection for her.

In certain situations you will help a girl, mother, or grandmother with her coat. It's helpful to stand behind her holding the coat at her waist level. She can then slip her arms in easily. Then gently pull it up to her shoulders. A nice touch if she has long hair is to lift her hair out of from inside her coat.

Hand kisses at the right moment with the right girl can be a gentlemanly, romantic and a charming gesture.

Always comfort a girl if she is crying. How?
Listen, empathize by nodding and ask the reason why she is crying. Some things you can say depending on the situation: "I understand this is painful for you", "I know it's a difficult time right now for you", " I know you're feeling hurt", "is there something that I can do?", "Can we talk about this some more?" "I am sorry this has happened to you.", How can I be of help…"

If appropriate and you're not crossing any lines she may be comforted by:
- A kiss her on the forehead
- Offering a hug
- Holding her hand
- Stroking her hair or arm
- Resting your hand on her forearm or shoulder

Defend your girls honor; don't let your friends talk bad about her. You also shouldn't talk negatively about her to your friends.

When a girl says the word "no" she means NO.

Don't share intimate details about your girlfriend with your friends.

Holding a girl's hand means that you care about her; she will probably like that.

On one of your dates, bringing a single flower or something sweet to give to her is a gentlemanly gesture.

Watch out for the bossy and controlling girls unless you want to be controlled. It does make your life easier if that is what you want.
Clue: check out how her mother treats her father.

If a guy asks a girl on a date, the guy should always pay for the evening. Once you have established a boyfriend and girlfriend relationship a girl can also treat. Who pays in the future is a conversation you need to have based on your incomes and abilities to pay.

If you go on a date and it doesn't work out and you don't intend on going on a second date with her, you should still pay. It shows you are a classy guy. In addition, you don't want the word to get around that you have a reputation of being cheap. (It's small world).

Please don't expect sex because you have paid for the evening out.
It's not a trade. Dating is not making installments for sex.

Watch out for the girls who are looking for a walking and talking ATM.

It's nice to offer your hand to help a girl.

Become a man your mother and grandmother would be proud of.

Help take the groceries in the house without being asked.

Dating is what you do until you find the girl you want to be in a relationship with. Then you stop dating and change your "single" Facebook status.

Know that most girls operate on a higher speed emotionally; it can be hard to catch up.

If the time comes and you decide to propose marriage: make it special and a memorable moment. Girls like to hint of marriage and some may even propose marriage to you.

Let the girl sit down first at the table when you are out to dinner.

In a social setting, always introduce your girlfriend to your friends or others. (Unless of course, you run into your ex-girlfriend then it may be uncomfortable).

Always have money in your wallet in case you need to tip the valet or coat check.

There is an unspoken rule floating out there of waiting 3-5 dates before having sex. If you really like the girl, it could be many more dates before you or she feels ready, if at all.

If a girl makes a special effort to dress up acknowledge it by telling her she looks nice. In fact, you should always tell a girl she looks nice when you see her.

Chapter 10

Become good friends with the person before you start a romantic
relationship, and love should follow.

You can't force love.
Someone can hide behind the word "love "to fool you
but, when they show you love,
you can see the words in action.

Something good is always worth waiting for and the longer you wait
the better it could be

Don't confuse good sexual chemistry with love; it's not the same thing.

Girls want to be your first and your last true love.

Fight for the girl you love... don't let her go!

Treat the girl you love as if she is the most important person in the world. She will treasure you in return forever.

Love is a gift there is no taking it back; you can only stop gifting.

If you fall in love with someone and they don't love you back, don't beat yourself up. There is nothing wrong with you. It sometimes happens. You could be the right guy it's just the wrong time.

If someone falls in love with you and you don't feel the same way be kind, gentle and honest but not hurtful. Don't take advantage of their love for you!

Love is something you feel and it's hard to explain.
Sometimes it may feel as if you can't imagine your life without the
other person, or your heart skips a beat in anticipation to see them
again.

Love is unlike, sex, love is a **process**.

Love can be shown in many different ways.

If all else fails, remember: whatever comes from the heart
is something you should never regret.

Love and sex are not the same...

Love and lust are not the same...

Having sex should be an intimate, deep and emotional connection that needs to be between two consenting adults.

"Hook-ups" are just a physical act of sex.

A lasting, and loving relationship will probably not start out as a "hook-up."

Please don't be afraid to love.
You might regret the chance you did not take...

Try not to over use the words "I love you".

Most girls need to hear "I love you" more often than guys.
They are just wired that way.

You need to give love to receive love.

The "In Love Feeling" is short lived. People are on their good behavior at first. They eventually will go back to who they really are. Then, the real work/joy of love starts. You need to remember and do the things that made you fall in love with each other initially and keep doing those things. If you don't keep doing them you can easily "fall out of love."

When you love someone you should try not to hurt their feelings.

Where there is love, there is unspoken trust.

"There can be no true love without trust."
~Elias A. Lianos

Don't be afraid to end a bad relationship because some need to end.

Love is doing something thoughtful and unexpected for the person you love.

When you love someone, you put their needs before yours.

When you are loved, you are high on your lover's priority list.

Love is giving her the last piece of chocolate cake you've been saving for yourself.

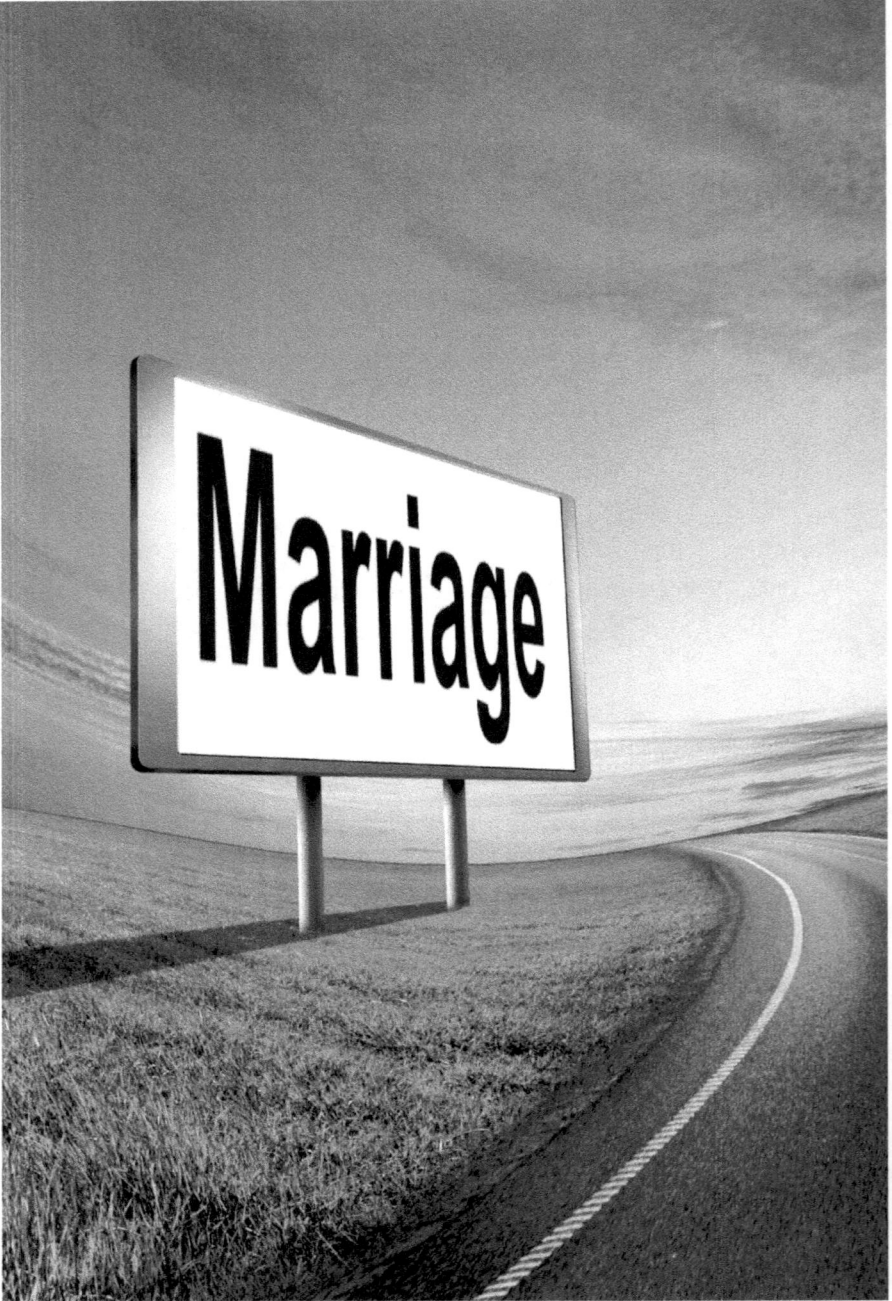

CHAPTER 11

Marriage is a partnership.
Think of it like this: One person is behind the steering wheel of a car,
and the other person navigates.
Ideally, you take turns driving and navigating,
but don't go over the speed limit,
and try not to get lost.

Marriage is a commitment.
Don't feel that you have to get married because all your friends are getting
married. Do it for the right reasons. Ask yourself why you want to get
married and why not stay single?

Marriage is a lottery: you never know who you will end up with and if you
have a winner.

When you're married you stay with the person unconditionally. They are
your "go to person" for love and comfort. It's the natural societal process
that once you fall in love you marry the person.

Try not to get caught up in the hype of a big, extravagant, and expensive wedding. Have a budget you can afford. Don't go into debt to fund your wedding. Your wedding day should not be viewed as a goal. Instead, the beginning of a new life with on-going goals to share with the person you love.

In a marriage, you need to work as team and be in alignment.

When you find your soul mate, be careful that you don't become roommates, and end up as cell mates.

Divide and conquer: chores should be shared.

In a marriage it's been traditionally the man's role to support and provide for his family. A woman should, however, contribute in other ways. It gets complicated and you need to work as a team.
Note: Unless she is a CEO of a fortune 500 company.

Communication in a marriage is critical and so is laughter.

Don't rush into marriage.
Get to know the person before making that commitment.

"Marriage is like a roller coaster... enjoy the ride"
~ Leo Melissourgos

Marriage is not all heavenly rainbows. It takes two people who make the decision to share one umbrella and survive the rain storm together.
Have a big beautiful umbrella on hand...

Marriage can provide comfort and security. It's sometimes the reason some people stay together.

CHAPTER 12

It's a sign of respect to knock on a closed door.
(Also, be prepared for what you might see or find on the other side if you don't knock).

Call whenever you are going to be more than five minutes late for an appointment or date.

Respect yourself and others will too.

Be willing to show love and care toward other people, even strangers.

"Find the best way to remember the names of the people you meet; especially while you're still talking to them."
~Daniel V. Gonzalez

85

Never break a promise. Otherwise, don't make one.
Promises are presents in advance.
"Pinky promises" also count.

Return voicemails, emails, and text messages. :-D

Show respect to everyone. It doesn't matter what job they have
or what type of work they do.

"Respect and love go hand and hand."
~Christos Voulikis

Take off your hat while eating dinner unless you're at a picnic.

When at a sporting event during the national anthem: stand up, put your drink and hotdog down and also please take off your hat.

Remember to always say "excuse me", "please", "thank you", and "you're welcome" too.

Sometimes people need a few seconds or hours to be alone with their thoughts. Respect the time they need or have requested from you.

Show respect for other people's feelings. Their feelings may not be the same as yours, but it doesn't mean that their feelings are not important or shouldn't be respected.

If you don't agree with someone else's opinion, it doesn't give you the right to disrespect him/her. You can agree to disagree.

Always wait your turn and don't skip.

If you are able to, offer your seat to the elderly or a pregnant woman.
This applies anywhere: a restaurant, an airport, or train station.

Don't interrupt others when they are talking, unless you ask their
permission.

Always make eye contact when speaking to someone.
If you are uncomfortable, looking at the bridge of their nose when speaking
to them makes it easier.

The tone and volume you use to communicate expresses the respect you
have for the person.

Telling the truth is a sign of respect.

Being respectful towards others shows you have good manners.

Having self-respect will take you places you'll want to go.
Having no self-respect may take you places you shouldn't go.

Respect should be non-negotiable.

Remember to pick up after yourself; the maid is on vacation.

CHAPTER 13

Respect other people's religion even if you don't agree with it.

"Don't pray for things. Pray for wisdom, courage, and guidance."
~Frank Gonzalez-1972

God sometimes speaks through the actions and voice of others.
(Psst...pay attention)

We meet people in our lives for a reason.
Some people may feel like God has sent them.
Free will lets you decide if you want them to stay or if you let them go.

Love Is patient, love is kind and is not jealous; love does not brag and is not arrogant, does not act unbecomingly; it does not seek its own, is not provoked, does not take into account a wrong suffered, does not rejoice in unrighteousness, but rejoices with the truth; bears all things, believes all things, hopes all things, endures all things.
1 Corinthians 13- New American Standard Bible (NASB).

Treat people the way you would like to be treated.

"Put your sword back into its place; for all who take up the sword shall perish by the sword"
Matthew 26:52- New American Standard Bible (NASB).
(Those who use violence will be a victim of violence)

"God helps those who help themselves."
(Aesop, Greek Story Teller)

"Talk less and pray more..."
~Bob Gountis

It's best to always forgive. Know that forgiving is not saying its ok...
Sometimes you just got to let it go.

Always love your brother and your sister too.

The recommendation and belief has always been to wait
until marriage to have sex.
If you decide not to wait until marriage, know that the person you have sex
with will share a soul tie with you.
Two bodies become one, and you will carry that soul tie forever.

"Faith is like Wi-Fi:
It's invisible, but it has the power to connect you to what you need."
(Unknown Author)

Prayer can be powerful.

The Holy Bible is the best-selling book of all time,
sold and gifted world-wide.

It's been noted and believed by many that the Holy Bible is the most stolen
book. This can make you wonder, why it's the most stolen book?

(It's also ironic because "thou shalt not steal" is one of the Ten
Commandments.)

"God gives nuts, but he does not crack them."
(Old Proverb)

God doesn't like laziness.

"God allows us to experience the low points of life in order to teach us lessons that we could learn in no other way."
~ C.S. Lewis

Believing in something is better than believing in nothing.

Chapter 14

While having dinner with others, try not to use your cell phone.

Focus on the person you are with, not your phone.

When in a meeting or an appointment, put your phone on vibrate or silent.

Remember not to use your phone in a public bathroom.
You never know who might be in the stall next to you.

Ask permission to view photos on someone's cell phone.
If he/she is only showing you one photo, it is not polite to scroll through
the rest or take over their phone.

Have a professional sounding ring tone or have your phone on vibrate
when at work. Follow the company's cell phone policies regarding when
you can use your phone. (Instead of talking on the phone, text if you can;
it's less distracting to others around you).

Remember to turn your cell phone on silent while watching a movie at the theater; it is very distracting to others around you if you don't and the phone goes off.

A good rule of thumb: if your call is disconnected, whoever initiated the call should call back first.

Remember that you or others may not understand the intent of a text because the tone of the words and body language are missing.

Please don't break up with someone over text.

If you are expecting an important call, let the person you are with know that, when the time comes, excuse yourself to take the call.

Have an important conversation in person,
not through a text or over the phone.

*I can't he-a-r
you... We're
b-r-e-a-king
up....*

*Huh, what...I...
didn't know we
were dating?*

CHAPTER 15

It might be cool at school, but the reality is that it's **NOT OK** to send naked photos via text or through apps like Snapchat. There are sexting laws that carry penalties. Even if you receive naked photos you should delete them off of your phone. If you save or store them and it's discovered by school authorities you will get in trouble. You could get suspended or expelled from school. This is considered pornography and you could also get arrested. Depending on your age you could get charged as an adult. Each state has its own laws and punishment.

Be careful when using apps on your cell phone for example: Kik, WhatsApp Messenger or Omegle. There are people who pose as someone they are not and try to manipulate you to do things you shouldn't.
Note: The Omegle app's terms and conditions states: "predators have been known to use this app". This is very scary!

Gaming and Computer Time~
Please don't spend too much on the gaming console. There is more to life than sports, zombies, missions and getting to the next level. Playing or spending too much time on a gaming console or other computer action type activities re-wires your brain and you're unable to find pleasure in real life situations. Playing video games causes over stimulation and can also make you lethargic and cause you not want to do homework, work or chores.

Pornography is a multi-billion dollar industry. It comes in different forms and degrees. It's a larger money maker than the NFL, NBA, and Major League Baseball combined. That's amazing, isn't it?

To provide a little history on the evolution of adult material: Playboy magazine was the first magazine featuring women in nude photographs (with great articles to read). However, the company has reported a decrease of 83% in sales as a result of the invasion of internet porn. In 2016, Playboy announced it is restructuring their magazine not to include nude photographs.

Viewing pornography online can cause the same re-wiring when playing on a gaming console. When a young guy's body is still developing so is his brain. Watching porn hijacks the sexual signal in your brain, takes you hostage and puts you on the wrong mission. Viewing on-line porn can become a serious addiction -if you're doing it, STOP! It messes with the chemicals in your brain and also associates images, ideas and reference standards about your partner that are not realistic. A person who views on-line porn can be seriously affected and could be missing out on true intimacy. They will not learn how to bond appropriately with another person. Watching internet porn doesn't provide love and affection. A person becomes de-sensitized. It's a very dark place that could cause depression, loneliness and isolation. It also creates unrealistic expectations in relationships, not to mention it degrades the view of women. It's a phenomenon that is becoming more prevalent in many younger guys and their world of electronics. Don't think for a moment that it's the same as magazines, VHS tapes or dial up service being viewed by the previous generations because it's not. This is HD (High Definition). It's more intense and virtual.
Don't be that guy!

WARNING: The websites you visit on your computer, smartphone, tablet or iPod are tracked even if you delete the browser history.

You shouldn't believe or trust everything you read on the Internet!

Remember that social media is public. Don't display yourself on Facebook, Twitter, Vine, Instagram or any of the other media out there if you don't want your boss, significant other, mother, father or the rest of the world to know your business. Social media is building a dossier on you!

Snapchats are deleted automatically, but they are also stored in the cloud. There is no guarantee that they are deleted within a certain time frame. In addition, this doesn't prevent someone taking a screen shot and saving or sharing the photo. Technology can be complicated and is constantly changing so you need to be aware of all this, the next time you snap.

I know it sounds CREEPY... but potential employers do look you up on social media to find out what kind of person you are.
It's easy to do: "google" your name and see what comes up.
Surprising, isn't it...?

Have you wondered what the cloud is? "The cloud" is a metaphor for "the internet". Something that is stored in the cloud means the information is located and accessed from a network of servers, instead of your computer's hard drive or cell phone. It's like a storage center. For example, when you store your photos on Dropbox or Google Drive you are storing them in the cloud.

When using social media represent yourself in the best light; otherwise it could embarrass you months or years later.

Remember: when you write emails, they are not private; they're stored in the cloud and can be printed.

Use a secure WIFI connection when possible because
it protects your information from being stolen.
The additional benefit of using Wi-Fi is that it saves on your data charges.

Re-read your emails, posts and tweets before you HIT the send button. (This is especially important if you are upset).

Remember not to share too much by tweeting every detail of your life.

If you are sending an email remember to add a subject in the subject line.

It's true; spell check doesn't always give you the correct spelling of a word. The auto correct feature on your cell phone can give you some pretty funny substitutions so re-read before sending.

Selfies can be a great expression and are fun to share. Don't overdo it. There have been accidents reported while taking selfies. Believe it or not, some people have inadvertently caused a car crash or even fallen off a cliff while taking selfies.

Keep your passwords safe, and DO NOT share them with anyone.
Try not use the same password for everything.
Change your passwords often.
I know it's a time consuming pain...

Don't enter personal data like your credit card or your social security
numbers if the website is not secure. It will have an "S" for secure in the
web address. (i.e. http**s**)

Protect your phone and other electronic devices,
and be careful of web surfers looking over your shoulder.
Note: They don't always wear Hawaiian surfing shirts.

If you get suspicious emails or voice messages, report it.

Be aware of "phishing". Phishing is a way of luring and the attempt to steal your personal information like user names, passwords and credit card information. Phishers are clever and masquerade as people from reputable and legitimate companies. They will do it over email, phone, or through social media.

Be aware of "spear phishing" attacks. They are emails that you receive from a "friend or business" that looks like it's really from them. They (hackers) know your name and use it in the email addressed to you. They can get your information from recent on-line purchases or from posts you made on social networking sites. Hackers will attempt to get your passwords. They also ask in the email for you to take action immediately or to open a document they have sent.

All this means keep up with technology.

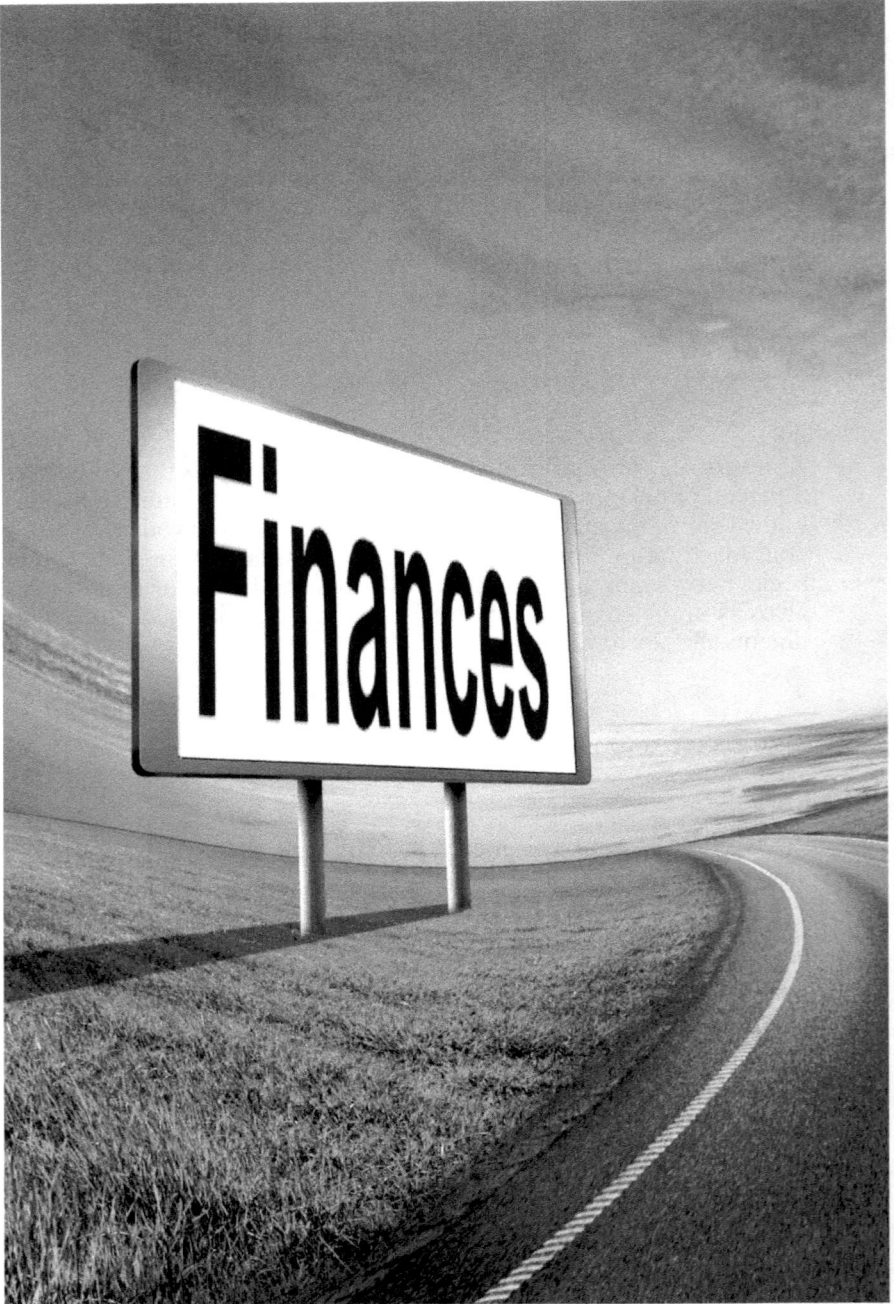

CHAPTER 16

When you turn 18 years old (WHOO HOO!), you become a legal adult. Don't sign your name on any contracts or documents without reading and understanding them. Don't be afraid to ask questions.

Your credit score starts at age 18. A credit score is a report card of how you manage your money. If you have a good report card, you are loaned money, and if you don't have a good report card, you might not be able to get a loan. It's calculated based on the history of how you pay your bills. If you pay them on time it helps your credit score positively. Also, paying on time avoids interest which is extra money you pay to the lender. You might not think this is important right now, but your credit history follows you for a long time. Your credit report is reviewed when renting an apartment, leasing or financing a car. Some employers, depending on the job you are interviewing for, will look at your credit score as a measure of your character and dependability.

You are responsible to pay your own debts or fulfill any agreements you have signed.
(Not your parents).

If you have "CC's" (credit cards), use them only for convenience.
All you really only need is one credit card, maybe two at most.
Try to pay the balance off every month.

Once you get out of school, have at least $200.00-$300.00 stashed at
home you never know if you will need it case of an emergency.
Hopefully you will never need it.

Try to save at least 10% of each paycheck in the bank or some type of an
investment.

You can learn to budget your money. Create a system, it could be an excel spreadsheet or even a note book. Write down how much money you have coming in and how much you have going out through bills and expenses. This provides a basis on how you spend your money and it helps you create a budget.

Save at least a 3 to 4 month salary once you start working as a backup. This is in case you have to change jobs or something unexpected happens and you need money to pay your bills.

When the time comes and you want to buy a house or condo, try to get a 15 -20 year mortgage. The shorter the term of the mortgage, the less amount of interest you pay. You will need a down payment which may be 10%-20% of the sales price. Interest is extra money you pay the bank or lender for the money that was loaned to you.
Why should the banks charge interest?

Keep a constant eye on the interest rates. You may want to re-finance your loan to avoid paying interest on the money that you borrowed. You can use that extra money to put towards your loan to pay it off in the same amount of time or less. If you are not good with numbers or finances ask someone who is.

"Bean by bean the sack gets filled"
(Saving a little bit at a time adds up)
(Greek Proverb)

If you're trying to save money look at the little things that you buy. Drinking coffee, latte's or other drinks daily at $4.00 a day adds ups. Let's do some simple math: $4.00 x 7 days a week = $28.00.
$28.00 x 4 weeks a month = $112.00
$112.00 x 12 months = $1.344.00 a year.

What could you do with that extra money?

When you want to buy something, ask yourself, do you really need it or do you just want it? Can you really afford it?

Remember to try and control your money, but don't let it control you.

Whoever pays the bills makes the rules.
Let your children know that if and when you have them.

Never count on someone else's money; make your own.

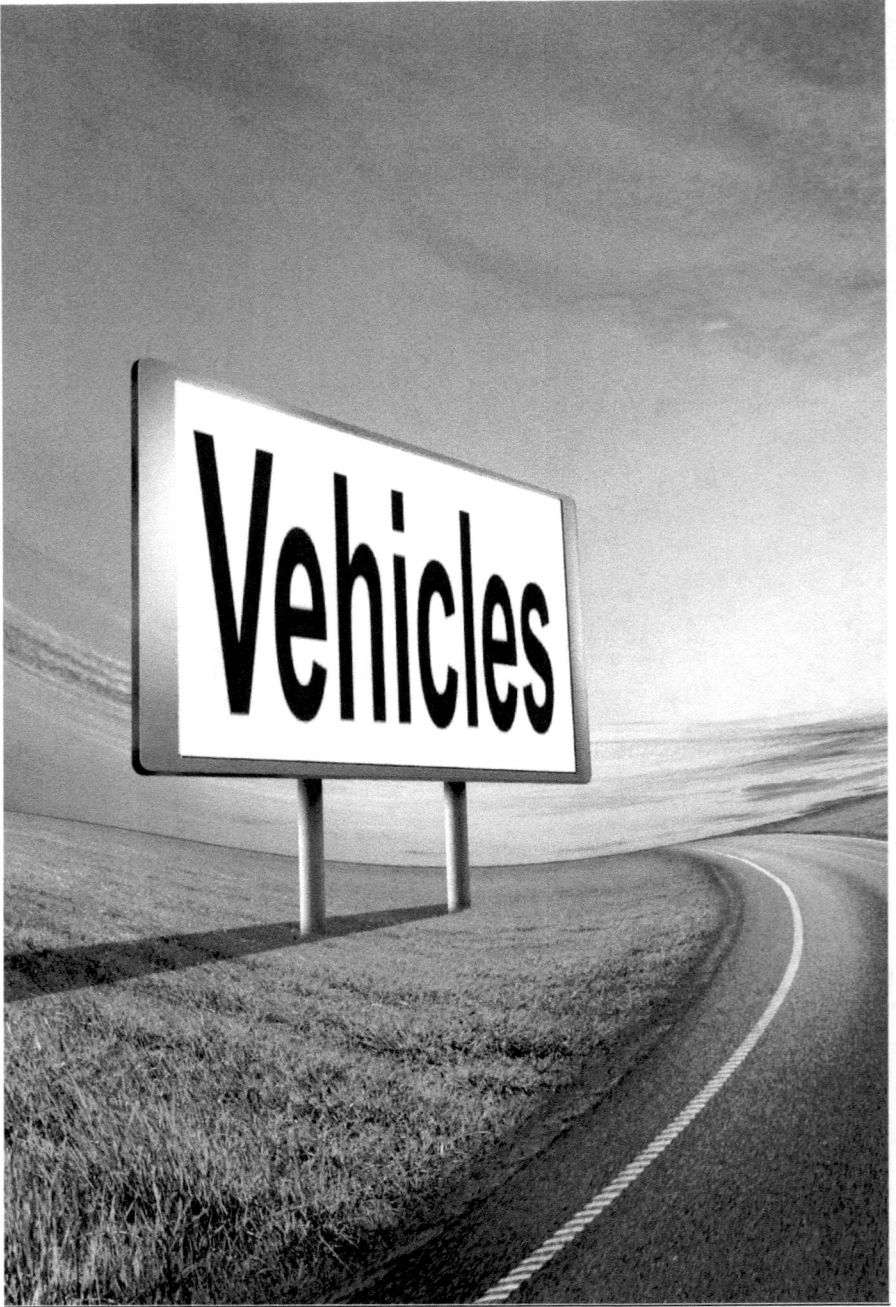

CHAPTER 17

"Have your parents review the rules of driving
before teaching you to drive."
~Amalia Melissourgos

Your car is one of the most expensive and important
possessions you will own. Take care of it.

Change the oil on your car at least every 3,000- 5,000 miles.
Also, learn how to check the fluid levels.

Buy new tires when you need them.

If your brakes start feeling or sounding funny,
don't wait to have them checked out.

Keep your registration and insurance card in the glove box.

If you get the opportunity to learn to drive a car with a stick shift, do it. It's fun and you never know when you may need to drive one.

Be an attentive driver.

Always wear your seat belt and request that your passengers do to.

Talking on the phone while driving is distracting, it doesn't matter if you are using hands-free or the speaker. You need to be focused on driving. In some states, you can be pulled over and ticketed for talking on your cell phone if you are not using a hands-free device. The best advice: don't talk on the phone while driving in any state.

When you borrow someone's vehicle, return it clean with a full gas tank.

PLEASE   DON'T   TEXT   AND   DRIVE!

Oh by the way...

PLEASE   DON'T   TEXT   AND   DRIVE!

Did I mention...

PLEASE   DON'T   TEXT   AND   DRIVE!

Have I said...

PLEASE   DON'T   TEXT   AND   DRIVE!

117

If you ever get pulled over by the police, stay cool. Roll down your window; keep both hands on the steering wheel until you are asked for your driver's license. Don't get out of your vehicle, unless you are asked to.
Be respectful and address the officer as sir.
You need to be honest and cooperative when asked,
"why do you think you were pulled over?"

If an unmarked squad car pulls you over and the officer asks you to get out of the vehicle, ask to see his/her identification. If your gut is telling you something doesn't seem right or you feel that you are in danger, call 911 to verify. The dispatcher will know if there is an unmarked squad in your area.

If you are in a rear end collision call 911 immediately and then your parents.

Get a second opinion or estimate on any car repairs.

Remember: park 15 feet away from a fire hydrant.

Changing the radio station in someone's car
without asking for permission can be annoying.

Learn to change the tire on a car.

Don't ignore the check engine lights on your car.

Always negotiate the price when buying a new or used car. You may feel
more comfortable taking your brother, uncle or father along the first time,
but only if they can help.

When buying a car, beware of the question.
How much are you willing to spend?
"They will try to sell the least amount of car for that amount of money."
~Daniel V. Gonzalez

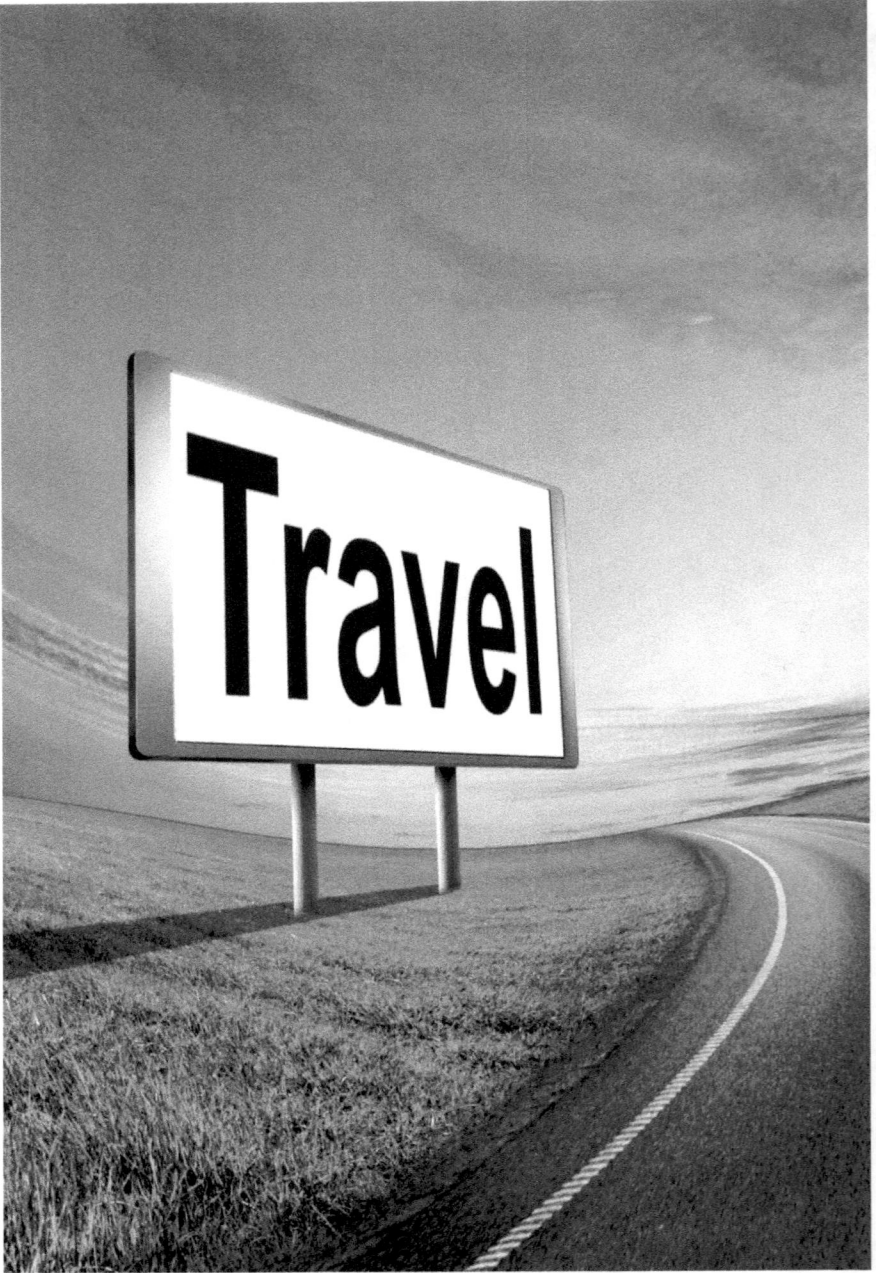

CHAPTER 18

If you have the opportunity travel and see the world.

Do some research on the location you plan to travel to.

Make a check list of items that you will need for the trip.

Have a change of under clothes, shirt, tooth brush and tooth paste in your carry on. Plane delays and lost luggage do happen, and it's nice to have those things on hand if it does.

Remember to pack that good pair of walking shoes.

"If traveling to a foreign country, learn about their culture, and some of their basic words for communication."
~Amalia Melissourgos

121

Check to see if you need a passport. If you already have one, make sure you re-new it several months before your travel dates.

Do you need immunizations prior to going to that country?

Check to see if you need an international driver's license, in case you would like to rent a car and drive in that country.

Contact your wireless provider and ask questions about the cellular service in the area that you are traveling.

Ask your wireless provider if you need to turn on or add a data package.

Will you incur roaming charges, if so what are the rates?

Does the hotel offer free Wi-Fi?

Before you leave for your vacation or trip, make your bed with clean sheets. It is nice to come home to your own bed with fresh sheets.

Leave your home tidy with dishes and glasses put away. Also, unplug small appliances like a toaster or coffee pot.

Keep your valuables on you or in backpack when in transit.

Never leave your things unattended!

When on vacation don't take off on your friends or leave them behind
for something that may seem better.

If you take a taxi cab, know that some taxi cab drivers may take advantage
of tourists by driving them around in circles to charge higher fares.

"If you're are converting or exchanging currency (money),
look at the fluctuating rates.
Each bank provides different rates and it varies day to day."
~Konstantinos Kokalis

Learn the exchange rate of the foreign currency especially when paying for
things. Sometimes tourists are taken advantage of by the owners of
restaurants or shops. Review the bill and the money you receive back from
your transaction. Also, remember to ask for a receipt.

Learn military time (24 hour clock) and how to convert it. An easy way to do so is by subtracting 12 from the 24 hour time. Example: 17:00 hrs-12:00 hrs. = 5:00 p.m.

Take a lot of photos.

"Make a photo album of your trip.
They are cool to look at and reminisce about."
~Amalia Melissourgos

Not everyone lives in a two parent home. It sometimes doesn't work out that way. Know that it's okay. You need to accept whatever situation you or your friends are in, and make the best of it.

Sometimes we don't understand why our parents do what they do... until later in life.

You are responsible for your own actions. You can't blame a bad situation entirely on your upbringing because you make the choice to be who you are and do what you do.

Parents and caregivers are teachers.

Remember that parents were once teenagers.
Shh...that's why they sometimes have insight on things.

Parents can make mistakes too; not all of them are *aliens*...

If you become a parent, it is one the most important responsibilities you
will ever have, and a life changing one too. Fasten your seat belt.

Please try to get to know your parents before it's too late!

"You spend years wishing your parents would get off your back only to realize they're the only ones who ever really had your back."
~Unknown author

There are role models all around you. Determine who the good ones are. You can also learn what not to do from the less desirable ones.

When your parent's age, which is inevitable, there are responsibilities that need to be taken care of. When you become older, you may need to have those tough conversations with them.

I still can't figure out where parents have hidden those eyes on the back of their head!

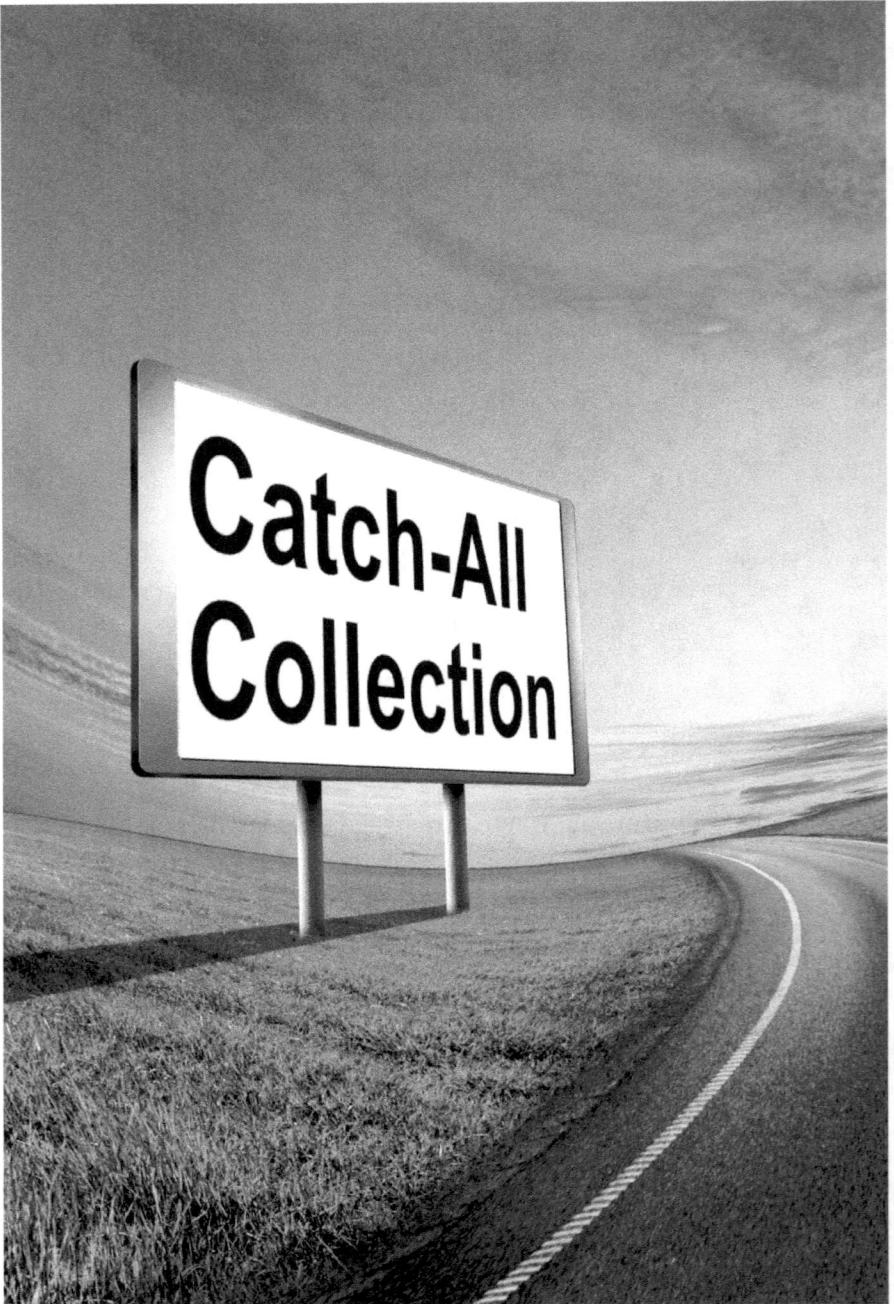

CHAPTER 20

"If you are depressed, you are living in the past. If you are anxious, you are living in the future. If you are at peace, you are living in the present."
-Lao Tzu

Sometimes you just have to live life one day at a time, to get over or work through whatever is troubling you.

Try to live your life without regrets. There will come a time you will reflect back on your life and you might regret the things you didn't do.

Voting is a right and a civic responsibility. Exercise your rights and vote. Trivia Note: In ancient Athens, those who were not participating in civic assemblies or not voting were called idiots and marked by red paint on their body.

Always do more than what is expected.

If you want to meet an interesting person, maybe you need to be
an interesting person.

People can basically fall into three categories: The maestros in life, the
observers in life, and the ones who wake up one morning and ask
themselves what the heck has happen to my life.
What category do you want to be in?

Adults go through stages in life; sometimes they last decades. They want a
big beautiful house and then they want to down size later in life.
Perhaps there is something to be said about adopting some of the
minimalist attitude early in life. Having a lot of material possessions can be
meaningless. Find what gives your life meaning and purpose.

"There is no right way to do the wrong thing."
(Unknown Author)

Be Confident; it's always an attractive quality to have.

Know there is a difference in having confidence and being arrogant.
(Some people who are arrogant are just insecure)

Live in the moment, but be responsible.

Never think that apologizing is a weakness.
It is strength to admit you are wrong.

Take a typing class.

International fun superstition: If you give a purse or wallet as a gift, always include a small amount of money inside. If you do, the person's wallet or purse will always be filled with money.

Most girls don't like guys who walk around a festival with their shirt off even if they have a six pack ab. Instead, show off your abs when its' appropriate.

Remember: when using a screwdriver; righty tighty, lefty loosey.

Have dreams and make them big!

Find what you are passionate about and do it!

Explore and try new things.

Sing in the shower!

"Learn Spanish."
~Leo Melissourgos

Sometimes in life you need to use the KISS principal:
"Keep it Simple Stupid" – (noted by the US Navy in 1960)
Or "Keep it short and simple."

Don't judge a book by its cover; you don't know the "inside" story.

"When you hear of many cherries, bring a small basket."
(Greek Proverb)

Don't live in clutter.

Have a robust vocabulary.

Learn to tell good stories!
Story telling has been around for centuries.

Try to avoid the four "hot" topics that can cause arguments:
sex, politics, money and religion.

If you find what you are passionate about, the hours will feel like minutes.

Always have a back-up plan when there is high stakes involved, and when
in doubt.

Harboring anger and resentment towards people is allowing them to live rent-free in your mind. Let them go, kick them out, or start charging them rent.

"Insanity:
doing the same thing over and over again and expecting different results."
~Albert Einstein

Try camping once in your life; breathe in the fresh air; close your eyes and enjoy the silence if only for a moment.

Take a chance; make a stance in your life. Fight for what you believe.

Have a cool signature.

Be organized with your thoughts and possessions.

You learn a lot from the drunk, the young, and the old because they have little or no filters which mean they speak the truth.

Have someone take you fishing once in your life. Fishing brings serenity and your stress dissipates. The exception when the fish start to bite.

Everything happens for a reason, but we might not know the reason or lesson until much later.

When you turn 18 you need to stop asking your mom and dad for their approval on the little things. You need to start making decisions on your own. This is not to say that you shouldn't ask for their opinion and guidance but ultimately you need to make your own decisions and accept the outcomes whether good or bad. This teaches you how to make decisions.

The familiar road is the one you have taken before and it may be shorter. The road never taken may be a longer one, but it's the one we learn the most from.

Learn to sew a button back on your clothing. If you can, sew it back on right away so you don't lose the button.

Choose wisely who share your bed with.

Plant a garden at least once in your life.

Gambling doesn't solve problems or make you richer. Gambling should be for purely entertainment purposes. Don't gamble if you don't have money to lose. The odds are you won't win your money back. Do you think that those beautiful casinos were built on people winning?

Learn to appreciate what you have; even if you don't have much there are others who may have less than you.

Keep a journal of your thoughts and dreams or anything worth remembering. Try to be disciplined and write daily.
It could be funny or inspiring to read years later.
Note: You might also decide to burn it later in life so your kids don't find and read it...

If you take the last cookie, don't leave an empty box in the cupboard.

"Even if you put your name on something to save for later, someone else might still eat it."
~Amalia Melissourgos

Volunteer your time and give back.

Think before you ink.
A tat is permanent.

The harder you work for something, the more you will appreciate it.

Life has so many twists and turns sometimes you need to be spontaneous.

Don't give others your garage code.
It's basically giving away the key to your house.

Learn to play golf. It's good exercise.

If you have nothing good to say, don't say anything at all.

Find a productive way to manage your stress.
It could be reading, writing or exercising.

It's perfectly ok to ask others for directions if you're lost.

Be a man of strong and good character.

Learn how to fix things. It's useful to be able to fix things that are broke
instead of paying someone else.

Own a tool box.

Read the directions included in the box.

Sometimes there is a need to scratch or adjust yourself; if you must do it,
be discrete.

Pay back all debts or money that has been loaned to you.

Return all things borrowed; that includes tools.

When a man gives his word that he will do something, he does it.

You shouldn't be asked twice to do anything.

Learn how to grill food.

Please don't drink directly out of the juice or milk container and put it back in the refrigerator.

Learn how to do laundry.

Make a bucket list of things you want to do, see, learn,
achieve and accomplish.
Start it now.

Always remember to kiss your mother on the cheek no matter how old you
are; she will like that.

Avoid physical violence; it solves nothing.
Walk away if you can; otherwise, do defend yourself.

Face your fears. Discover your strengths. Know your weaknesses.

"A journey of a thousand miles must begin with a single step."
~Lao Tzu

Some parents buy and fill your backpack.

Some parents only buy or only fill your backpack.

Sometimes parents don't know how to fill a backpack.

There is nothing wrong with any of this,

and during your lifetime you should keep filling it yourself.

If you have the chance, try filling someone else's too.

About the Author

Elizabeth earned a Bachelor of Science in Social Welfare from the University of Wisconsin-Milwaukee. She worked as a social worker after graduating and also volunteered her time in several non-profit organizations. After a short time in the field, she pursued a career in sales. Elizabeth works in the wireless communications industry as a successful business sales professional and has been with the same company for over 25 years. Her experience included serving in both management and non-management roles during her career.

www.ingramcontent.com/pod-product-compliance
Lightning Source LLC
LaVergne TN
LVHW021344080426
835508LV00020B/2104